ORIGAMI
FOR
BEGINNERS

The Creative World of Paperfolding

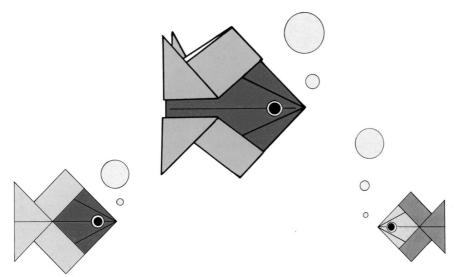

Florence Temko

Charles E. Tuttle Company
Rutland, Vermont & Tokyo, Japan

Acknowledgments

Many thanks to Lillian Oppenheimer, Founder of the
Origami Center of America, for offering her strong
and warm support for this book, to Yolanda and Tyler
Anyon, V'Ann Cornelius, Mark Kennedy, Martha Landy,
Jeanne Lynch, Remy O'Connell, Carole O'Connell,
Joyce Rockmore, Janet Temko, and to the participants
in my origami classes at the San Diego Museum of
Art for testing the instructions. Thanks to the Friends
of the Origami Center of America, the British Origami
Society, the International Origami Society, the Nippon
Origami Society, and the many other associations
that keep enthusiasts like me informed about origami
activities all over the world.

The Car is based on a design by Kosho Uchiyama;
the Gift Box was designed by George Jarschauer; the
Furniture Units are based on designs published in
Pasteless Construction with Paper by Marie Gilbert Martin
(New York: Pageant Press, 1952). The following de-
signs and their applications have been created by
the author: Pine Tree, Trick Mouse, Napkin Blossom,
Squawker Toy, Cat, Skyscraper, Space Rocket, Napkin
Ring, Barking Dog Puppet, Bell Flower, Pilgrim's Bon-
net, and Robot.

Published by the Charles E. Tuttle Company, Inc.
of Rutland, Vermont & Tokyo, Japan
with editorial offices at 2-6 Suido 1-chome,
Bunkyo-ku, Tokyo 112

©1991 by Charles E. Tuttle Publishing Company

LCC Card No. 91-65237
ISBN 0-8048-1688-3

First edition, 1991
Fifth printing, 1997

PRINTED IN SINGAPORE

CONTENTS

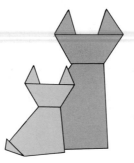

INTRODUCTION

Origami, the art of paperfolding, is fun and easy! Even if you've never folded paper before, you'll find the objects in *Origami for Beginners* easy to make. As you flip through the pages of this book, you'll surely spot something that interests you. Even if it looks difficult, it's really not, so go ahead and give it a try. Let's say you find the Elephant especially appealing. If you follow the step-by-step directions carefully, you'll get good results. And when you fold the Elephant a second time, you'll discover that you can make it even better and faster than the first time.

Origami is believed to have originated in China, but the craft developed most fully in Japan. For centuries, Japanese origami was closely associated with traditional ceremonies, but over time, the craft became a popular family pastime. In recent years, origami has spread all over the world to such an extent that origami clubs have sprung up in many countries. Through these clubs, origami enthusiasts meet regularly, hold exhibitions, and disseminate information through newsletters and other publications.

While origami is an ideal activity for children, many adults have discovered that paperfolding is a creative, challenging, and relaxing hobby. Some paperfolders have created designs that are widely recognized as valuable works of art.

Like any other craft, origami is based on a few fundamental techniques. Before you begin folding, be sure to look over the next section, Practical Information, so that you're familiar with these simple yet important origami guidelines.

Symbols

The folding symbols in this book conform to a system used by paperfolders throughout the world. For the most part, the symbols are self-explanatory and can usually be followed even without referring to the written instruction.

Fold in this direction

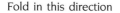

Fold along this line

- - - - - - - - - - - - - - - -

Existing crease

_____

Valley fold—fold toward you to create a valley

Mountain fold—fold away from you to the back; this creates a mountain (Always check whether you're making a valley fold or a mountain fold.)

Fold under another flap

◄ - - -

Illustration has been enlarged

⇨

Turn back to front, i.e., turn origami over

Model

One completed origami figure.

Base

Basic starting point for making different models. Three bases are shown in this book: the Blintz Base, Kite Base, and Diamond Base.

Paper

Most of the models in this book are made from square pieces of paper with widths of between 6″ and 10″ (15 and 25 centimeters). If a special size or kind of paper is needed for a particular model, this is clearly specified. Prepackaged origami paper, which usually is colored on one side and white on the other side, is handy to use. Unless specified otherwise, the directions in this book are for paper that is colored on one side only. You can, however, experiment using other types of papers. All crisp, fairly thin papers such as gift wrap, or bond, computer, or stationery papers are suitable for origami. When you cut paper to a desired size, be sure that you cut it into exact squares or rectangles.

Some projects look better when folded with double-sided origami paper—either special origami paper that has different colors on the front and the back, or ordinary paper, like stationery, that happens to be colored on both sides. You can also make your own double-sided paper by pasting together different papers, and then cutting to the desired dimensions.

ORIGAMI
FOR
BEGINNERS

BLINTZ BASE, QUICKY GIFT ENVELOPE, LAYERED CARD, LAST-MINUTE GREETING CARD

BLINTZ BASE [Use any square]

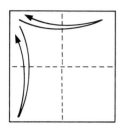

1. Fold in quarters. Unfold.

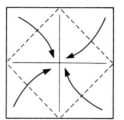

2. Fold corners in.

3. Blintz Base.

QUICKY GIFT ENVELOPE [Use a 10" or larger square of gift wrap]

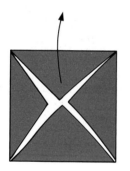

1. Fold a Blintz Base. Open one flap.

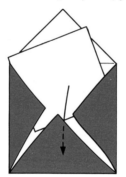

2. Insert a card, a scarf, stamps, money, or other flat gift.

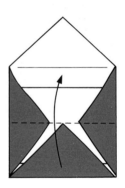

3. Fold bottom edge up.

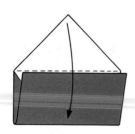

4. Fold down flap.

5. Quicky Gift Envelope.

The Blintz Base

The Blintz Base is named after a pastry that is made by taking a square of dough and folding its four corners to the center. Using this easy Blintz Base as a starting point, you can fold many different models, several of which are shown here.

LAYERED CARD [Use three squares: 4", 5", and 6"]

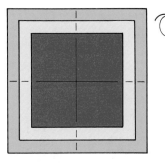

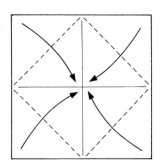

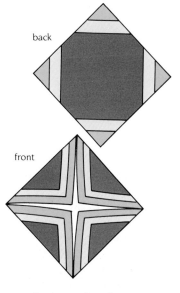

back

front

1. Fold each square in quarters. Unfold. Center squares and glue, one on top of the other. Turn back to front, so that largest square faces up.

2. Fold corners to middle.

3. Layered card.

LAST-MINUTE GREETING CARD [Use a square of gift wrap]

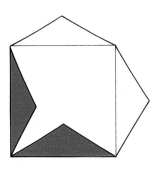

1. Fold a Blintz Base. Open flaps and write greeting inside. Close flaps.

2. Add a sticker to seal the card.

CHRISTMAS STAR, STAR EARRINGS, GIFT WRAP DECORATION, CAR

CHRISTMAS STAR [Use a 4″ square of double-sided paper or foil gift wrap]

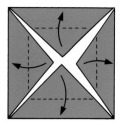

1. Fold a Blintz Base. Fold all corners to outside edges.

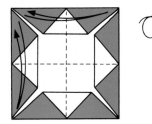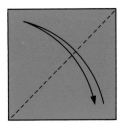

2. Fold in quarters. Unfold. Turn back to front.

3. Diagonally fold in half. Unfold.

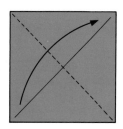

4. Diagonally fold in half again. Leave folded.

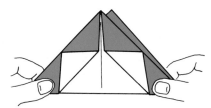

5. Grasp opposite corners. Push into a star shape.

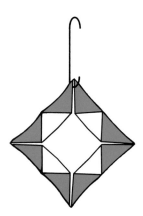

6. Christmas Star. Attach an ornament hook.

STAR EARRINGS [Use two 2″ squares]

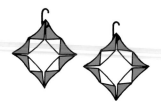

Fold two Christmas Stars. Attach earring fittings (refer to Jewelry, p. 46).

GIFT WRAP DECORATION

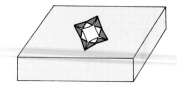

Apply glue to the edges of the back of a Christmas Star and place on a package.

The Car

The Car shown below can be made, with minor changes, into many types of cars—family cars, racing cars, even antique cars. The directions here show how to make a car using a square, but you can make a longer, sleeker model if you use a rectangle.

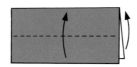

CAR [Use any square]

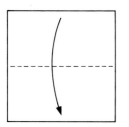

1. Fold in half.

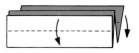

2. Fold front flap up.
   Fold back flap up.

3. Fold front flap down.
   Fold back flap down.

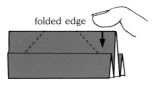

4. As shown, push top center fold down between side folds until corner extends below bottom. This makes a wheel. Repeat at opposite end to make other wheel.

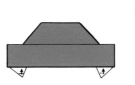

5. Fold up bottom corners of wheels. Turn back to front.

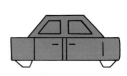

6. Car.

KITE BASE, PINE TREE, TRICK MOUSE, FANTASTIC FLYER AIRPLANE

KITE BASE [Use any square]

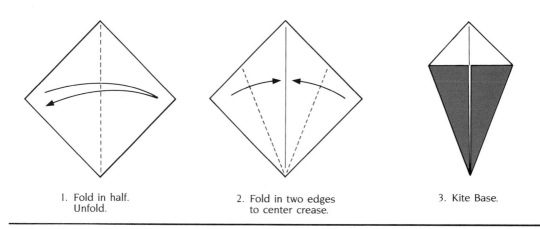

1. Fold in half. Unfold.

2. Fold in two edges to center crease.

3. Kite Base.

PINE TREE [Use a green square]

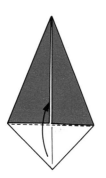
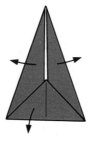
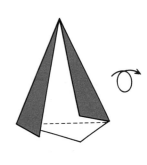

1. Fold a Kite Base. Place as shown. Fold up triangular flap.

2. Loosen all three flaps.

3. Turn back to front and place tree upright.

4. Pine Tree.

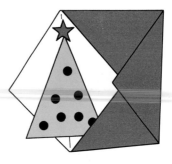

For a unique Christmas card, flatten Pine Tree and send with a note explaining how it can stand upright.

TRICK MOUSE [Use a 2″ square]

1. Fold a Kite Base. Fold in half by bringing one triangle over the other.

2. Trick Mouse. Tap tail to make mouse jump.

   For better action, make very sharp creases. Gluing the bottom two triangular flaps together will also help.

FANTASTIC FLYER AIRPLANE [Use any square and a paper clip]

1. Fold a Kite Base. Turn back to front.

2. Fold edges in.

3. Mountain fold in half (refer to Practical Information, p. 6).

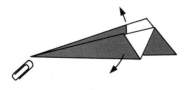

4. Place wings at 90° to the body. Attach a paper clip to the nose.

5. Fantastic Flyer Airplane. Throw airplane upward.

EARRINGS, ICICLES, SUNBURST, NAPKIN BLOSSOM

EARRINGS [Use two 2″ squares]

1. Make two Airplanes (p. 13).

2. Attach earring fittings. Earrings.

ICICLES [Use 4″ squares of foil gift wrap]

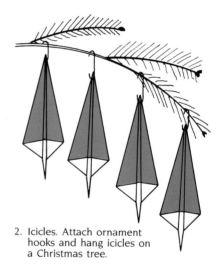

1. Fold Airplanes (p. 13).

2. Icicles. Attach ornament hooks and hang icicles on a Christmas tree.

SUNBURST [Use large, bright yellow squares]

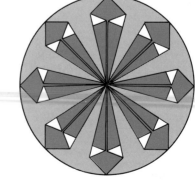

1. Fold eight Airplanes (p. 13), stopping at step 3.

2. Glue in a circle on a posterboard. Sunburst.

Table Settings

With very little effort, you can fold lovely paper or fabric napkins that will enhance any dinner table. Placing these Napkin Blossoms in glasses will add an extra touch of elegance. You can also create a truly impressive table setting by using napkins to make a Sunburst.

NAPKIN BLOSSOM [*Use a paper or fabric napkin*]

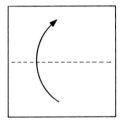

1. Fold in half.

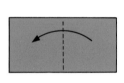

2. Fold in half again.

four corners here

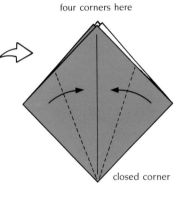

closed corner

3. Place as shown. Fold a Kite Base (p.12).

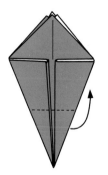

4. Mountain fold bottom corner to back.

5. Mountain fold in half.

6. Place in glass. Pull down outside three corners one at a time. Napkin Blossom.

DIAMOND BASE, SQUAWKER TOY, SHARK

DIAMOND BASE [Use any square]

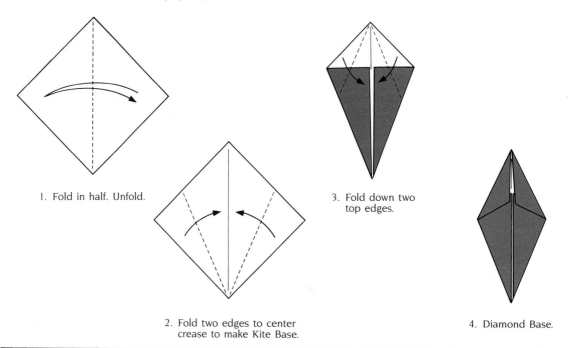

1. Fold in half. Unfold.

2. Fold two edges to center crease to make Kite Base.

3. Fold down two top edges.

4. Diamond Base.

SQUAWKER TOY [Use any square]

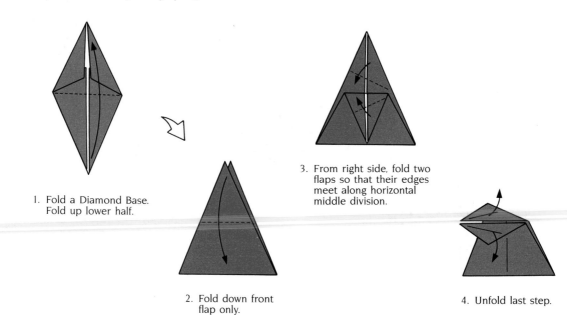

1. Fold a Diamond Base. Fold up lower half.

2. Fold down front flap only.

3. From right side, fold two flaps so that their edges meet along horizontal middle division.

4. Unfold last step.

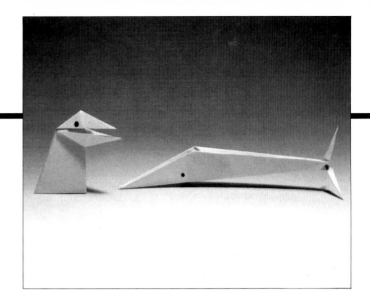

Party Favors

From 10″ squares, make one Squawker Toy for each place setting. Both young and old will be delighted with these adorable birds. Use bright colors to fold the Squawker Toys and staple strips of colored paper to both sides of their backs to create fancy tails.

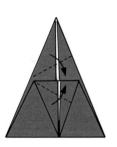

5. From left side, fold two flaps so that their edges meet along horizontal middle division.

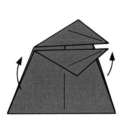

6. Mountain fold bottom half of paper in half; let Squawker's beak settle naturally into creases made in steps 3 and 5.

7. Squawker Toy. Pull sides apart to make beak open.

SHARK [Use any square]

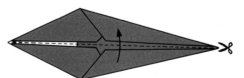

2. Make small cut at long, narrow end. Fold in half.

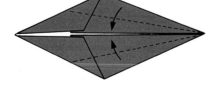

1. Fold a Diamond Base. Fold edges in.

3. Fold one tail fin up, the other down. Shark.

CAT, STANDING CAT, CAT FAMILY

HEAD [*Use any square*]

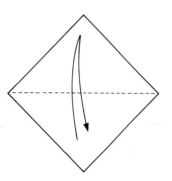

1. Diagonally fold in half. Unfold.

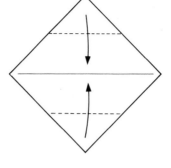

2. Fold corners to center crease.

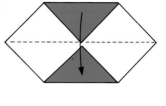

3. Fold in half.

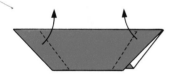

4. Fold up sides.

5. Turn back to front.

6. Head.

BODY [*Use any square*]

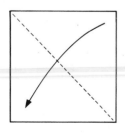

1. Diagonally fold in half.

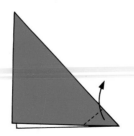

2. Fold up to make tail.

3. Body.

Cards and Notepapers

Cat lovers everywhere will enjoy receiving gifts, letters, invitations, and holiday cards decorated with these origami cats. You might want to experiment using different types of colored and patterned paper, and drawing in eyes, nose, and whiskers with a felt tip pen.

ASSEMBLY

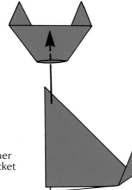

1. Insert top corner of Body in pocket of Head.

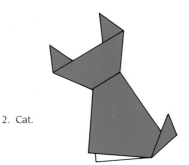

2. Cat.

STANDING CAT [Use any square]

The Cat stands up if you unfold the tail, open the whole body, and wrap the tail around the front and back while closing the body. This procedure is called an "outside reverse fold."

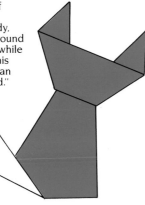

CAT FAMILY [Use 4", 6", and 8" squares]

To make kittens, use two 4" squares. Then make the adult cats using 8" squares for the bodies and 6" squares for the head.

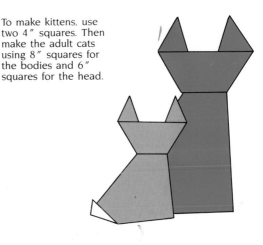

GIFT BOX, COVERED BOX, EASTER BASKET

GIFT BOX [Use any square]

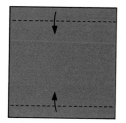

1. Place colored side up. Fold in two edges of equal widths.

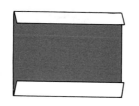

2. Turn back to front.

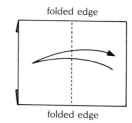

folded edge

folded edge

3. Fold in half. Unfold.

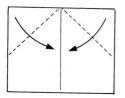

4. Fold corners in.

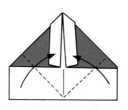

5. Fold corners in.

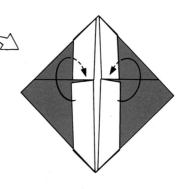

6. Tuck bottom cuffs into top cuffs.

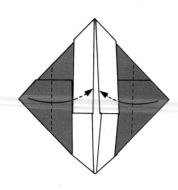

7. Fold corners under cuffs.

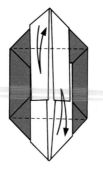

8. Fold top and bottom corners in. Unfold.

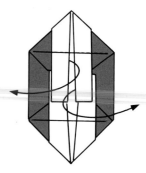

9. Open box by lifting up cuffs.

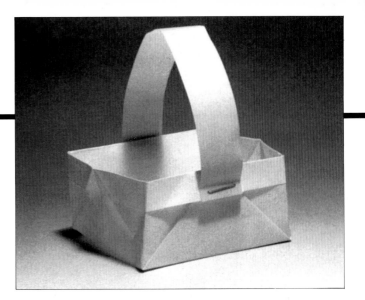

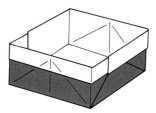

10. Sharply crease corners at 90° angles. Gift Box.

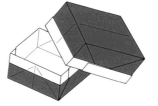

COVERED BOX [Use two squares]

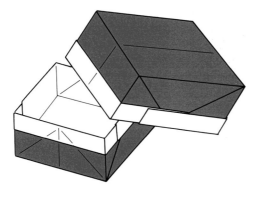

Fold two Gift Boxes, one from a square about 1/2″ smaller than the other. The larger box will serve as a lid for the smaller box.

EASTER BASKET [Use a square and a strip of paper]

Fold a Gift Box. Cut a strip of paper and fold it lengthwise in half for a handle. Staple or tuck the ends under the cuffs of the box. Strengthen the basket by cutting a piece of cardboard the same size as the bottom of the box and placing it inside.

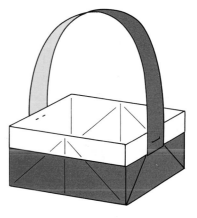

SKYSCRAPER

[Use about a 3″ × 11″ strip of paper]

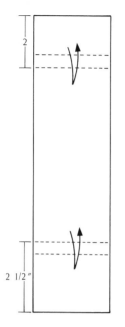

1. Make pleats by folding mountain and valley folds, i.e., fold flaps down, then back up.

2. Unfold two top creases.

3. Fold up two small corners.

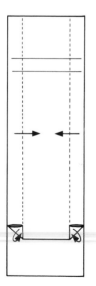

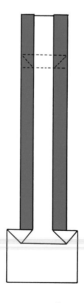

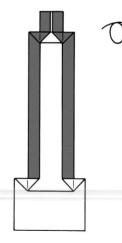

4. Open two small corners, and squash flat while folding side edges in. Two triangles should form at base of tower. Don't fold lower part of paper.

5. Once more, pleat top creases. Repeat steps 3 and 4 with two small corners near the top.

6. Turn back to front.

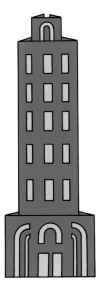

7. Skyscraper.

Hate Measuring?

With models such as the Skyscraper, there is no need for precise measuring. Simply judge by eye where you want to make the pleats.

Different Buildings

Vary the skyscrapers by changing the distances between the pleats, by adding more pleats, and by using different sizes of paper. Cut out pictures of the Empire State Building and other skyscrapers and use them as models.

Diorama

Make a city skyline on a bulletin board or a large poster board. Paste on or draw in trees and other landscape features.

SPACE ROCKET, NAPKIN RING OR PHOTO HOLDER

SPACE ROCKET [*Use about a 3″ × 11″ strip of paper*]

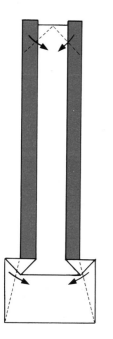

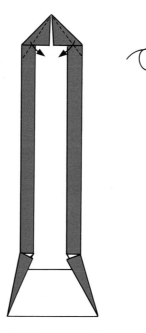

1. Fold a Skyscraper (p. 22) but make only the bottom pleat. Fold corners in at both top and bottom.

2. Fold top corners in. Turn back to front.

3. Space Rocket.

NAPKIN RING OR PHOTO HOLDER
[*Use about a 3″ × 11″ strip of paper*]

Fold a Skyscraper (p. 22) but make only the bottom pleat. Bend into a circle and glue or tape together in a place that cannot be seen. For a Napkin Ring that also serves as a place card, write a name on the square front. To use as a Photo Holder, simply affix a photo to the front.

24

Space Rocket *p. 24*, Sunburst *14*, Cat *18*, Layered Card *9*.

Layered Card *p. 9*, Cat *18*, Pine Tree *12*, Christmas Star *10*, Sunburst *14*.

Covered Box *p. 21*, Star Earrings *10*, Earrings *14*, Easter Basket *21*.

Squawker Toy *p. 16*, Napkin Blossom *15*, Pirate's Hat *40*, Car *11*, Napkin Ring *24*.

Flower Arrangement *p. 35.*

Chair *p.37*, Dining Table *39*, Bed *39*, Side Table *37*, Bell Flower *34*, Leaf *35*.

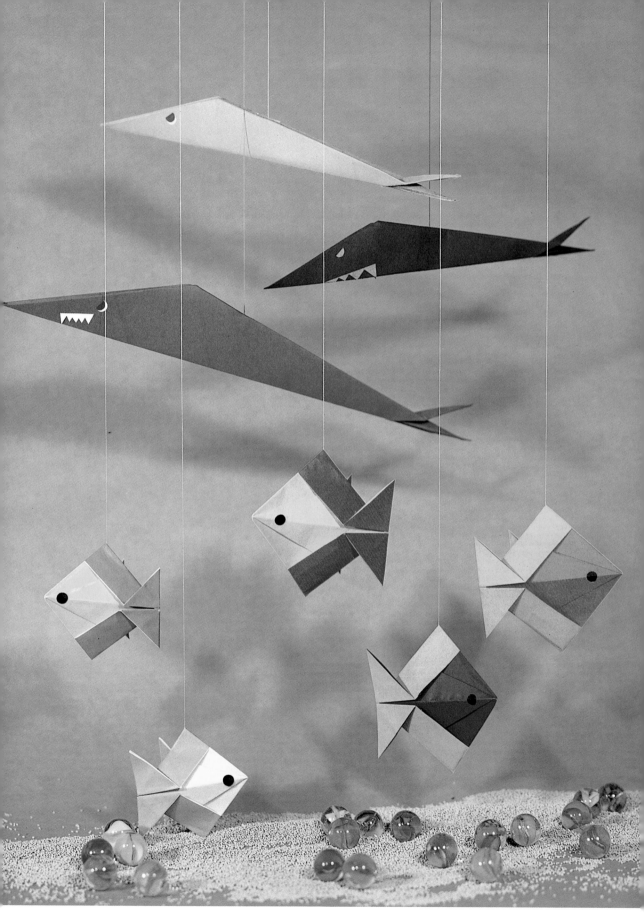

Shark *p. 17*, Tropical Fish *41*.

Elephant *p. 42.*

BARKING DOG PUPPET

[Use an 8" × 3" strip of paper]

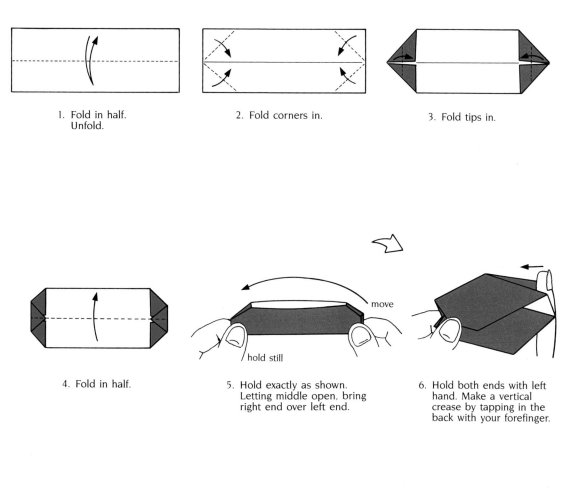

1. Fold in half.
   Unfold.

2. Fold corners in.

3. Fold tips in.

4. Fold in half.

5. Hold exactly as shown.
   Letting middle open, bring
   right end over left end.

move

hold still

6. Hold both ends with left
   hand. Make a vertical
   crease by tapping in the
   back with your forefinger.

7. Flatten paper by stroking
   from left to right with
   your thumb and forefinger.

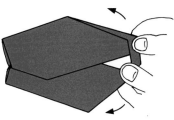

8. Barking Dog Puppet. Grasp
   lower flaps with hands.
   Move hands apart to open
   mouth, adding barking sounds.

HELP!
If step 5 proves diffi-
cult, first pull the paper
over the edge of a table
to make the spine flatter
and more pliable.

Make puppets for guests
to play with during a
party. Or, teach them
how to make the puppets
themselves.

BELL FLOWER, FLOWER ARRANGEMENT

BLOSSOM [Use a 3″ square]

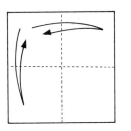

1. Fold in quarters.
   Unfold.

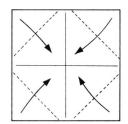

2. Fold four corners
   not quite to center.

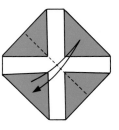

3. Fold in half.
   Unfold.

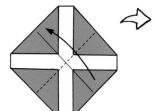

4. Fold in half.
   Leave folded.

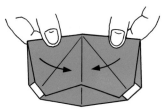

5. Grasp at folded
   edge. Push together.

6. Arrange petals at right
   angles to each other. Snip
   tiny bit off top corner.
   Blossom.

STEM [Use covered floral wire, 22 gauge recommended, or pipe cleaners]

ASSEMBLY

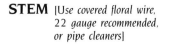

Cut wire to desired length.
Using pliers, roll one end
of the wire. Stem.

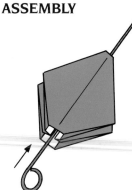

1. Insert unrolled end of
   wire in blossom so that
   it comes out cut end.

2. Gently bend stem so
   that blossom droops
   down. Bell Flower.

FLOWER ARRANGEMENT

Place your Bell Flowers in a vase or present them as a bouquet to someone special. For a truly unique and impressive display, use the flowers to make a beautiful, formal flower arrangement, as shown here.

MATERIALS:
  Floral wire or pipe cleaners
  Adhesive tape (floral tape sold at garden shops recommended)
  Plastic foam or floral foam (oasis)

LEAF [Use a 2″ × 4″ strip of green paper]

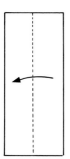

1. Fold in half.

2. Cut out oblong semicircle.

3. Unfold. Tape wire to bottom. Leaf.

ASSEMBLY

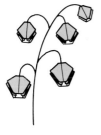

1. Make several Bell Flowers and tape their stems to floral wire, one above the other.

2. Cover foam with green paper and place in a shallow vase, bowl, or basket. If necessary, hold in place with floral clay. Insert flowers and leaves.

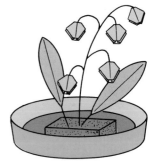

3. Flower Arrangement. You can also vary the size of the blossoms, and place the smaller blossoms above the larger ones.

FURNITURE UNITS I
BASIC UNIT, CHAIR, SIDE TABLE OR FOOTSTOOL

BASIC UNIT [Use two 6″ × 4″ rectangles]

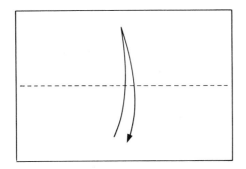

1. Fold first rectangle in half. Unfold.

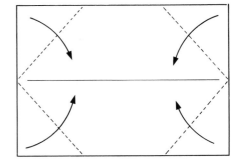

2. Fold in all corners.

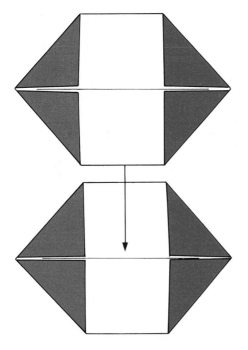

3. Repeat steps 1 and 2 with second rectangle. Slide one rectangle halfway over the other.

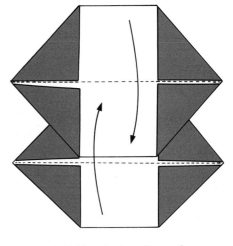

4. Fold up bottom flap, and then fold down top flap.

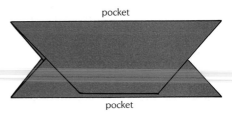

pocket

pocket

5. Basic Unit. The two pockets on the top and bottom edges are used to combine units. If you don't have two pockets, make sure the flaps in step 4 were folded one over the other.

Origami Furniture Pieces

These origami furniture pieces are perfect for dollhouses and for making architectural settings. You can make different sized furniture by using larger or smaller pieces of paper; be sure, however, to stick to the specified proportions. Construction paper is especially good for making these units.

CHAIR [Use four 6″ × 4″ rectangles]

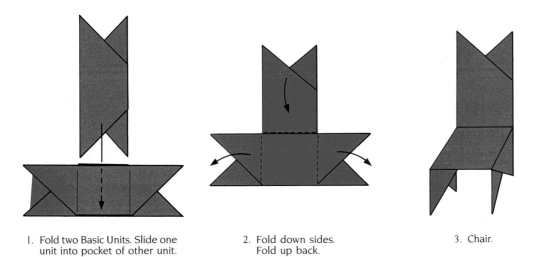

1. Fold two Basic Units. Slide one unit into pocket of other unit.

2. Fold down sides. Fold up back.

3. Chair.

SIDE TABLE OR FOOTSTOOL [Use two 6″ × 4″ rectangles]

1. Fold a Basic Unit. Fold sides down.

2. Side Table or Footstool.

FURNITURE UNITS II
BENCH, SOFA, BED, DINING TABLE

BENCH [Use two 8″ × 4″ rectangles]

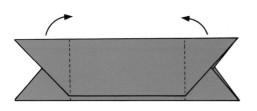

1. Fold a Basic Unit.
   Fold down sides.

2. Bench.

SOFA [Use three 8″ × 4″ rectangles]

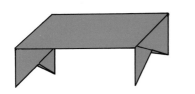 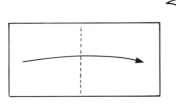 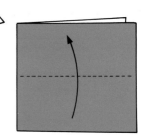

1. Use two rectangles
   to fold a Bench.

2. Fold third rectangle
   in half.

3. Fold in half again.

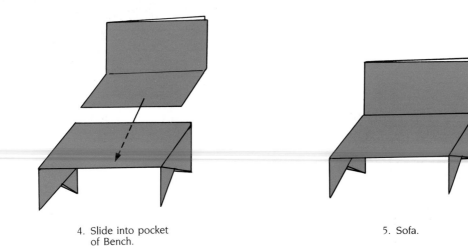

4. Slide into pocket
   of Bench.

5. Sofa.

Creating New Models

You can create many different models by thinking of these Furniture Units as versatile building blocks. With a little imagination, you can make flowers, butterflies, jewelry, greeting cards, puzzles, and three-dimensional pictures by combining them in a variety of ways.

BED [Use five 8″ × 4″ rectangles and one 6″ × 4″ rectangle]

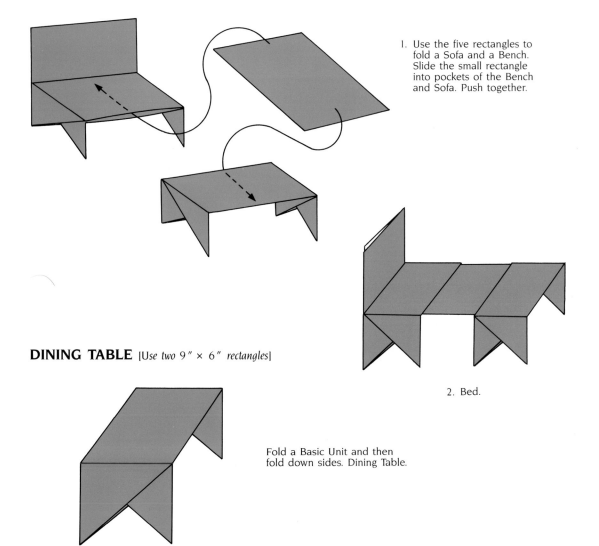

1. Use the five rectangles to fold a Sofa and a Bench. Slide the small rectangle into pockets of the Bench and Sofa. Push together.

2. Bed.

DINING TABLE [Use two 9″ × 6″ rectangles]

Fold a Basic Unit and then fold down sides. Dining Table.

PIRATE'S HAT, PILGRIM'S BONNET, ROBOT, TROPICAL FISH

PIRATE'S HAT [Use any square]

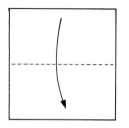

1. Fold in half.

folded edge

2. Fold in half. Unfold.

folded edge

3. Fold corners down.

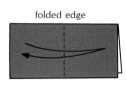

4. Fold flaps out.

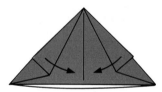

5. Unfold.

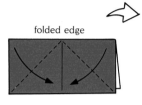

6. Poke finger into bottom opening of left flap. Swing flap up, and following creases, flatten. Repeat with right flap.

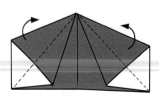

7. Mountain fold to back.

8. Fold up front flap as far as possible. Repeat on back.

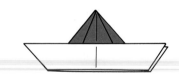

9. Pirate's Hat.

Squash Fold

Steps 4 through 6 of the Pirate's Hat make up a common folding technique called a "squash fold." As the name implies, the paper, guided by creases, is squashed into the desired fold.

Wearable Hats

Use a 23″ square for an adult's hat or an 18″ square for a child's hat. Fold with newspaper, gift wrap, wallpaper, or construction paper, and decorate the finished hat with feathers, paper cutouts, and stickers. Attach string or elastic to make a chin strap.

Aquarium

Tropical Fish and Sharks (p. 17) may not always be friends in nature, but they can be in an aquarium. Try inventing other kinds of origami fish by varying the folds, and experiment using the leaf design (p. 35) to make water plants.

PILGRIM'S BONNET [Use any square]

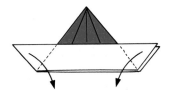

1. Fold a Pirate's Hat. Fold front pointed flaps down.

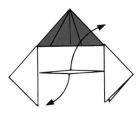

2. Grasp front and pull out slightly to the right; at same time, grasp back and pull slightly backwards to the left. Flatten.

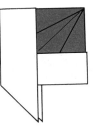

3. Pilgrim's Bonnet.

ROBOT [Use any square]

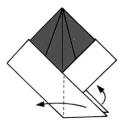

1. Make a Pilgrim's Bonnet. Separate two front flaps by folding top flap back. Repeat on back.

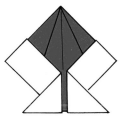

2. Robot.

TROPICAL FISH [Use any square]

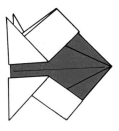

For a Tropical Fish, make a Robot and turn it sideways.

ELEPHANT

HEAD [Use any square]

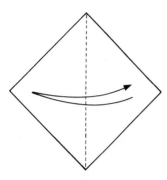

1. Fold. Unfold.

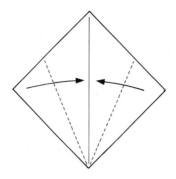

2. Fold edges in to center crease. (This makes a Kite Base.)

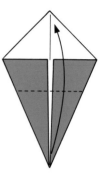

3. Fold up.

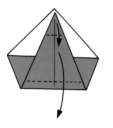

4. Fold tip down. Fold down again to form a pleat.

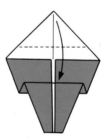

5. Fold top corner to the pleat.

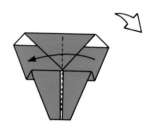

6. Fold in half.

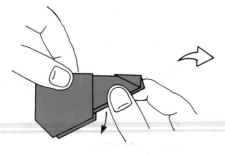

7. Pull down trunk. Make trunk stay in place by pressing area around the ear.

8. Pull away tip of trunk and press in place. Head.

Shaping

To make the head rounder in shape, try mountain folding all the corners. Or instead of making mountain folds at the top corners of the head, you can make "reverse folds"—folds formed by pushing the corners in between the two layers of paper.

Mammoth Elephant

Fold an Elephant from 36″ or larger squares of construction paper. Reinforce finished model by gluing pieces of cardboard in places where they cannot be seen.

Jewelry

Make small Elephants, gluing the bodies and heads together. Laminate with coatings of white glue and use as earrings and broaches.

BODY [Use any square]

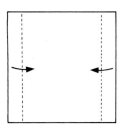

1. Fold in two edges.

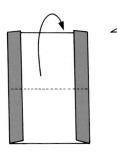

2. Mountain fold in half.

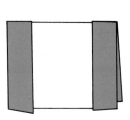

3. Body.

ASSEMBLY

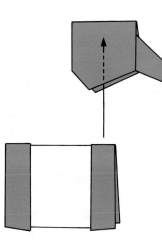

1. Open both body and head slightly. Slide body into pleat behind the trunk.

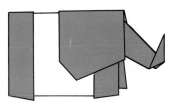

2. Elephant.

BOAT, SAILBOAT BASKET

BOAT [*Use any square*]

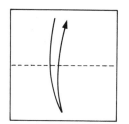

1. Fold in half. Unfold.

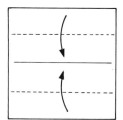

2. Fold edges in.

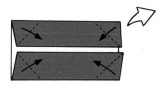

3. Fold four corners in.

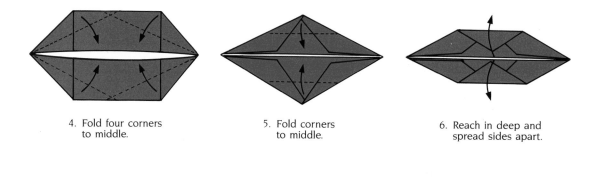

4. Fold four corners to middle.

5. Fold corners to middle.

6. Reach in deep and spread sides apart.

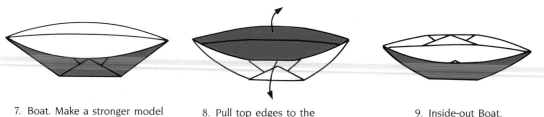

7. Boat. Make a stronger model by returning to step 1 and starting with the colored side up. Proceed to step 7.

8. Pull top edges to the outside while pushing up bottom of boat, turning it inside out.

9. Inside-out Boat.

Bathtub Frolic

These paper boats float, but they last longer if they are made from waxed paper. To strengthen them even more, staple their sides.

SAILBOAT BASKET [*Use an 8″ square and a 2″ × 10″ rectangle*]

1. Make a Boat from the square.

2. Fold rectangle in half.

1/2″ folded edge.

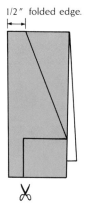

3. Cut out a sail. Leave 1/2″ of folded edge remaining at top of sail.

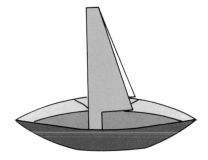

4. Staple sail to inside edges of boat. Sailboat Basket.

Origami Display Case

Create an origami display case by making origami models, cutouts, and hand-drawn illustrations, and then gluing them inside a large box (you may want to use the box shown on p. 20). For instance, you can construct a seascape by lining the inside of a box with blue construction paper, and then pasting in origami boats, sharks, and fish. You could also make a lid to cover the display for transporting it from one place to another.

Masks

Make masks by folding the head of the Cat from large pieces of paper. Pierce holes at the sides and attach string or elastic. Cut out holes for the eyes and mouth. You can also make masks with the Tropical Fish and the Elephant.

Jewelry

Fold the Bell Flower, Elephant, Tropical Fish, and other origami models from very small pieces of paper, and attach earring fittings or pin backings. Applying a coat of white glue to the models will strengthen them as well as give them a lustrous finish.

Earring fittings can be purchased at hobby or craft stores. You'll find different fittings for both pierced and unpierced ears. Instead of using ordinary fittings, you can pierce a hole at the top of a model, thread it with string, and tie a loop that can then be hung around the ears.

Origami Box

Construct a sturdy gift box using stiff paper such as art or construction paper and then fill it with origami. This makes a wonderful gift, especially for a sick child who is confined to bed.

Gift Wrapping

Paste the origami models on packages to create eye-catching gift wrap.

Oversize Models

Make dramatic works of art by folding models with large, heavy paper. Such paper is readily available at art stores; some recommended brands are Strathmore, Canson, or Ingres.

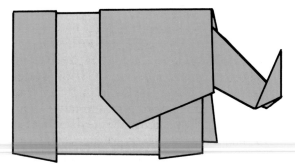

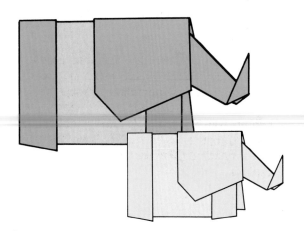

PAPERFOLDING IN SCHOOLS

Origami can help students improve their command of a variety of basic skills; for this reason, many primary and secondary school teachers use origami as an educational tool in the classroom.

How to Teach Origami

When teaching origami for the first time, start out by first thoroughly familiarizing yourself with the folding directions of a few simple origami models. Then, teach the models to students step by step. After students have mastered these easy models, you might find that they are able to proceed on their own by following instructions in a book or handout.

Art

Origami is an art medium that has some very attractive features; it uses material that is readily available, it doesn't make a mess as crayons and paints do, and it offers students an opportunity to create three-dimensional objects. Furthermore, origami improves eye-hand coordination, deepens visual, spatial, and tactile understanding, and stimulates artistic talent.

Math

It is interesting that many origami enthusiasts are scientists, mathematicians, and computer programmers. From my experience, I have found that gifted math students are also naturally skillful paperfolders.

On the other hand, teachers have found that origami can be an effective tool for teaching math to students who are *not* gifted in the subject. Origami can be used, for example, to demonstrate angles. By folding a corner of a piece of paper toward a center crease, you can graphically demonstrate the division of a 90° angle into two 45° angles. To children, unfolding origami models and finding triangles, rectangles, and other geometric shapes is simply fun, but while they are playing, they are learning to recognize basic shapes. With a little imagination, you can use paperfolding to demonstrate symmetry, proportion, geometric theorems, and other math principles.

Reading Skills

Folding paper can also help students improve their reading skills because it develops their perception, comprehension, and sequencing abilities. Origami also gives them practice in following directions. When telling stories, many librarians, teachers, and parents use simple origami animals, furniture, and other models to illustrate their narration. Another effective method is to have children make their own origami models, then have them verbalize or write about their creations.

Social Studies

Introducing origami to students learning about Japan, China, Spain, and other countries where paperfolding traditions have existed for a long time helps stimulate interest in the cultures of these important nations.

Special Education

Children with learning disabilities are often attracted to paperfolding. In fact, many specialists incorporate origami in their programs, and some have reported astonishing results when working with students with impaired hearing. Origami is particularly effective in helping to build the self-esteem of students with learning disabilities.

Free Time

Providing origami books and paper squares to students who have finished their assigned work keeps them quietly occupied.

Group Projects

A large-scale zoo, wildlife diorama, circus, farmyard, city skyline, or spaceship mobile—these are just a few examples of group projects that encourage cooperative learning. Children will take pride in displaying their finished projects on a school bulletin board, or in donating them to local libraries or hospitals.

INDEX

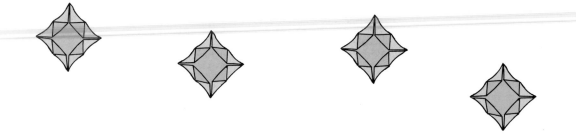